C000145660

Purple Ronnie's

Little Guide to

Getting Married

by Purple Ronnie

First published 2004 by Boxtree
an imprint of Pan Macmillan Ltd
Pan Macmillan, 20 New Wharf Road, London N1 9RR
Basingstoke and Oxford
Associated companies throughout the world
www.panmacmillan.com

ISBN 0 7522 7273 X

9 8 7 6 5 4 3 2

A CIP catalogue record for this book is available from
the British Library.

Text by Giles Andreae
Illustrations by Janet Cronin
Printed and bound in Hong Kong

Choosing Your Partner

Finding someone who you want to spend the rest of your life with can be one of the hardest things in the world

The Proposal

Remember - girls always like it if you propose to them in a romantic way

incorrect
correct
chuffed
Will you marry me my beautiful wonderful angel?

<u>Asking the Dad</u>

Sometimes it is polite to ask the girl's dad if you can marry his daughter

⭐ Try not to get too drunk before you do this

I just wanna... hic... shay that your daughter's... burp... really sexy... and... well
hic
fume
sway
tap
v. unimpressed

Telling the Families

When you first tell your families that you are going to get married everyone will go completely bonkers

Mothers-in-Law

Remember that your new mother-in-law has usually spent at least 20 years waiting for this moment

⭐ She will have some opinions

Your New Family

When you get engaged you will suddenly find that your fiancé's family is much bigger than you ever thought it could be

...urm pleased to...
hello dear
hic
... and this is Great Aunty Mavis... and 2nd cousin Dorothy ... and little Timmy of course
I can see your pants!

Shopping

Getting married is one of the best excuses ever for buying loads of new stuff

The Stag Night

If you like waking up naked, handcuffed to a lamp post in a pile of sick then you will LOVE your stag night

The Hen Night

Girls' nights out are one of the most frightening things ever invented

⭐The Hen Night is the scariest of them all

Pre-Wedding Nerves

You will probably wonder at least once whether you are really doing the right thing

☆ Don't Worry – this is perfectly normal

But, I'm just not sure he's really. y'know, THE ONE
hic
blub
BISCUITS

The Big Day- MEN

There are only 2
things you need to do:-

1. Turn up

2. Bring a ring

The Big Day- GIRLS

Everyone will spend the whole day telling you how amazing you are and how beautiful you look

⭐Enjoy it!

What to Think When You See Your Bride in Her Dress

" How could I ever live without you, you vision of pure loveliness ? "

What Not to Think When You See Your Bride in Her Dress

"Why did that thing cost so much when you look like a giant Christmas cake and you'll never wear it again?"

Crying

If you blub when you are saying your vows, everyone else will blub like mad as well

Best Man's Speech

It is traditional for the best man to try to embarrass the groom as much as possible in his speech

but he couldn't get it out of the donkey for 3 whole days!
oh no!
cringe
good heavens!
guffaw
!

The Wedding Night

Be careful not to tear
your wife's new undies

She will never have such
expensive ones again

The Honeymoon

After the wedding, the honeymoon is your big chance to have the most expensive holiday ever

hello, we're on our honeymoon
can we have an upgrade?
No
v. excited
CHECK-IN

Honeymooning

You are meant to Do It like mad when you are on honeymoon, but usually you are so fagged out after the wedding and the flight that all you want to do is sleep

Coming Home

When you get back
you will realise that
you have blown all the
savings you ever had,
but never mind...

...you have promised
to love each other
whether you are rich
or poor for the rest
of your lives so...

LOVE
and
BE HAPPY!